The killing of Officer Friendly

By

Lawrence Hutton

TABLE OF CONTENT

Introduction

In 1982 I graduated from Meade Senior High School and went straight into the Army a week after graduation where I spent 7 years, I have been every were from Fort Carson Colorado, Vincenza Italy, Demark, Germany, and Turkey. Within that time, I have learned and have seen a lot. Let me be the first to tell you if you ever have a chance to see the world or another country do it. In my last 4 years I lived in Italy before I finally left the military. After that I did a couple of odd jobs before a friend suggested I go into Law Enforcement. My first 7 Years in Law Enforcement was with the Easton Police Department in Talbot County Maryland. There I was a patrol supervisor and in the

COPS Unit, all prior to my departure. I had to leave there because of way too many “ISIMS” Favoritism, Nepotism, Racisms. In April of 1996 I left there for another Police Department and have been there for over 26 years. In my over 30 years I have seen it all and heard it all and yet there is always something that still surprises me. I have a lot of life experience, and knowledge, but it came with a price. I have also lost relationships, Marriages, family, and friends. People have no idea what it is like being a Law Enforcement Officer. There are those who believe that the police can do the same thing as what they see on television. I had a man who wanted me to fingerprint a Cinderblock. I told him I could not do it, and his response was “Well I saw it on television.” The only people who know or understand Law Enforcement Officers are those who are married to an Officer, or their family member is an Officer. The civilian world has no idea how difficult it is to be a Police Officer. I've heard some from the Entertainment World **Tweet** "We know it's hard, but you guys could do better." Let me tell you something, unless you have fought a 6' foot 4" 310lbs man on PSC, you have no idea how hard my job is. I intend to shed light to what it is really like and what a Patrol Officer must deal with daily. A Police Officer, not some News person, some Dean teaching Social Studies at a community College, some Politian or Conservative all of them only speaking their perspective about Law Enforcement. Always remember, a Police Officer is dealing with the broken part of Society, we see the victim or suspect at their worst, and the way police officers are being used and deployed by the government has also created an alienation with Law Enforcement and the Community.

I am writing this for many reasons. One reason is I know that much of the public needs to know what it entails to be a police officer. I am also writing this hoping that the public will be more willing to work with and be receptive of police officers and that the public can understand that at the end of the day we are human just like everyone else. Yes, I also know that there are bad Cops out there I do not doubt it, I have met them personally. I have met an officer who tried to bait me to do something for him to arrest me even after they knew I was a Police Officer. The title "The Killing of Officer Friendly." I came up with this title from a pleasant encounter I had with a woman one. She stated, "Hello Officer Friendly." And that was the time when things started to change in how patrol officers' police. Then I replied, "Officer Friendly is dead, he was killed making a traffic stop."

Let me make this clear in this book, the comments and statements are solely my comments and statements based on my experiences as a Police Officer and does not reflect that of my agency and other police officers.

Chapter One
Law Enforcement

Law Enforcement has existed for more than 200 years. Great Britain first created the Police Force prior to the Revolutionary War. Law Enforcement did not appear until years later. The Nottingham City Police, in England was also the first departments to use and develop the portable radio system. This system was developed under the direction of one Constable Captain Athelstan Popkess who was also responsible for the creation and development of the "Mechanized Division" from 1930 to 1959. In 1830 America adopted the first centralized municipal police departments:

Boston Police Department- 1838

New York City Police Department-1845

Chicago Police Department-1851

New Orleans / Cincinnati Police Departments-1853

Philadelphia Police Department-1855.

Newark New Jersey / Baltimore City Police Departments- 1857

By 1880 all major cities had a municipal police force in place. The reason was the explosion of major cities and urban areas in the United States and to curb lawlessness and maintain order. In the south police were used in slave patrols. The first was in the Carolina Colonies in 1704. In my first book ***"From Cotton to Crack."*** I explain in better detail how the south used its police to maintain control on slaves and Black people. It is said that one of the reasons Police were created in the United States was to regulate the control and movement of Slaves which has truth to the claim, not until the 1900 did the Law Enforcement Officer came to life. Finger Printing began in 1900 followed by the Crime Lab in 1920. The 911 system came online in 1960. Since then, Law Enforcement has grown and changed throughout the years, in both good and bad ways. Since its birth law enforcement has taken on people of color,

Women, and technology. Even with the so-called era of transparency the public still does not understand the goings on within a Police Department. No one knows what that Police Officer departmental policy, training, and law enforcement officer's authority are. What an Officers does or does not do. The public only knows what they see on television and social media which unfortunately never tell the truth or whole story. Let us start at the beginning. The word Police, it has many meanings.

Police

Noun

Police

Definition of *police*

1a: the department of government concerned primarily with maintenance of public order, safety, and health and enforcement of laws and possessing executive, judicial, and legislative powers

b: the department of government charged with prevention, detection, and prosecution of public nuisances and crimes

2a: POLICE FORCE

B plural: POLICE OFFICERS

3a: a private organization resembling a police force campus police

B plural: the members of a private police organization

4: one attempting to regulate or censor a specified field or activity the fashion police

5a: the internal organization or regulation of a political unit through exercise of governmental powers especially with respect to general comfort, health, morals, safety, or prosperity
b: control and regulation of affairs affecting the general order and welfare of any unit or area
c: the system of laws for effecting such control

6a: the action or process of cleaning and putting in order
b: military personnel detailed to perform this function

Police (Verb)

policed, policing

Definition:

1: To control, regulate, or keep in order by use of police

2: To perform the functions of a police force in or over

3 (a): To supervise the operation, execution, or administration of to prevent or detect and prosecute violations of rules and regulations
(b): To exercise such supervision over the policies and activities of

4: To make clean and put in order

Police Officers are intended to be the arm and extension of the government be it Federal, State, County, or Municipality of that jurisdiction to enforce the Laws of that county state and these United States. The Police Officer is the first direct contact the American Citizen has with the Government and the judicial system outside of politicians during election time. The citizen also must remember that the Police Officer is only a part of the Criminal Justice System as a whole. The Justice System has many parts. The following is a brief break down on how the system operates.

Police duties and responsibilities

- Maintain a constant presence in the community through regular patrols to deter crime and provide quick help when needed.
- Secure crime scenes and protect evidence from tampering or loss.
- Attend public events as security to help ensure peaceful attendance.
- Help identify potential crime spots and activities which may result in criminal acts.
- Remain vigilant regarding potential hazards or problems which could harm the public.
- Issue citations for traffic and similar violations.
- Apprehend those suspected of committing crimes.
- Write daily reports of activities.

Corrections Officers duties

Enforce Rules and keep Order: Inside the prison or jail, correctional officers enforce rules and regulations. They maintain security by settling disputes between inmates, preventing disturbances, assaults, and escapes. Officers enforce regulations through effective communications and the use of progressive sanctions, which involve punishments, such as loss of privileges.

Supervise the Activities of Inmates: Correctional Officers supervise the daily activities of inmates, ensuring that inmates obey the rules. They must also always ensure the whereabouts of all inmates. Officers also escort prisoners between the institution and courtrooms, medical facilities, and other destinations.

Search for Contraband Items: Officers search inmates and their livings quarters for contraband, such as weapons and drugs. In addition, an officer is responsible for screening visitors and incoming mail to ensure contraband is not brought into the prison or jail.

Inspect Facilities to Ensure that they Meet Standards: Correctional officers periodically inspect facilities. They check cells and other areas for unsanitary conditions., contraband, signs of a security breach (such as tampering with window bars and doors), and any other violations or the rules.

Aid in Rehabilitation and Counselling of Offenders: As many prisons and jails are often incredibly understaffed, correctional officers with advanced training or college educations are often utilized in the rehabilitation and counselling of offenders, in addition, correctional officers also participate in the rehabilitation efforts by scheduling work assignments, counseling, and educational opportunities.

Prosecutor Responsibilities

- Working with police officers and court staff.
- Instructing and advising counsel in court.
- Liaising with criminal justice and law enforcement agencies.
- Ensuring that criminals are punished fairly.
- Screening criminals.
- Handling appeals.
- Preparing criminal cases for pre-trial and trial.

Judges Enforce Court Procedure

The judge's first role is to make sure all the parties and witnesses follow proper court room procedure. Although this does not sound particularly exciting, procedure is of vital importance to the legal system. It was designed to ensure that everyone who comes to court gets a fair trial. In such circumstances, the judge is usually ruling on the part of procedure that governs evidence. The jury is only allowed to see or hear certain evidence so that they are not unfairly prejudiced toward (or against) one party. Although many questions about evidence are settled before the start of trial in pre-trial motions, sometimes these decisions have to be made on the fly while court is in session.

Judges Decide Issues of Law. Most trials have two arguments going on at the same time. The first is the argument over the facts of the case: who did what, where, and when? The jury usually decides these questions, although in some types of cases the judge can function as fact finder. The second argument is about the law. Each party's lawyer will study the laws written by the legislature and past cases to determine the exact status of the law. Then, the lawyers argue with each other about why the law favors their respective clients. Sometimes, when both parties mostly agree on the facts, this happens during summary judgment. When the facts are in dispute, the judge will provide the jury with instructions about the law so that the jury can make an educated decision about the case.

Court Commissioner

- Reviews applications for charging documents from all law enforcement agencies and private citizens, determines whether probable cause exists, prepares charging documents, and selects trial dates.
- Conducts initial appearance hearings for those detained on warrants, bench warrants, or on view arrests for the purpose of determining bail, incarceration, or release; identifies defendants in National Crime Information Center to obtain criminal histories; releases such defendants on personal recognizance or incarcerates them in default of bond.
- Determines the amount of bail to be set for each chargeable offense, accepts bail, property, cash, or corporate, issues commitments to detention center if

arrestee is ineligible for bail or is unable to comply with bail established.

- Advises arrested persons of their constitutional rights and the procedures required.
- Answers inquiries from the public and directs them to the proper judicial or law enforcement agency.
- Provides information to callers regarding operations, policies, and procedures governing the Judiciary's operations.
- Obtains material from a variety of sources to be used for articles, reports, and speeches.

The reason I put this part in is that a lot of people have a misconception of the how police officers and the criminal justice system works. Yes, police are called to the cat in the tree and the neighbor complaint of a loud kid's birthday party, but is that really what a Law Enforcement officer were meant to do? I believe that yes, the Law Enforcement Officer is the liaison between the government and the public and in the beginning meant to deter crime and arrest the felon. Then there came a time when someone decided that the Police Officer should be Officer Friendly and that officers should not only fight crime but also,

Direct Traffic be a....

Teacher

Lawyer

Counselor

Big Brother

Big Sister

AAA

Referee

Arbitrator....to name a few...

You can take any job anywhere on the planet and there is no other job that has as many responsibilities as a Law Enforcement Officer. For example, in my department, they require that each squad carries a dog pole to catch loose dogs which means we now do the job of Animal Control, we are now dog catchers. When I first came on the department all I had to do was call animal control, they would respond and take the dog away. Now I'll called the dispatcher to request an Animal Control Officer and their response is, "We'll come out when the Officer has the dog contained." So does this mean if an Animal Control Officer pulls up on a robbery in progress and calls 911, I can have the dispatcher tell him "Ill respond when you have the criminal in handcuffs." This is not a complaint I am just making an observation. There was a time that if there was a loose dog Animal

Control would respond and take the dog back to the pound. Now I get calls from child protective services to go by a residence and check on a child, again back when I first came on agents from child protective service went out and personally check on a child. I had an agent from child protective service call me telling me she received a complaint of a 15-year-old girl who had not been to school in 3 years, yes 3 years, and that her mother was soliciting her for sex. So, my first questions to her where did you call the school to verify the girl's attendance? "Well no." Well, when was the last time you saw her? I asked. Well, I have not seen her, I just got this case file. Ok why don't you just go by and check? Well, I do not see what the problem is. She stated. I've call police before, and they have just gone by to check. Well, I told her, I have been here going on 24 years and any time I have gotten a call from child protective service they have wanted us to meet them at the home or they are already there, and they are about to remove the children from the home. So, what you are telling me, I said, is that you want me to do your job, go by and check and then call you back at your office then you write it in your monthly report? Well, I am busy. Well, what do you think I am? I replied. We are even in civil matters, note police officers have no authority over civil matters. When a tenant has not paid their rent, the police were called to collect. Sorry the police are not a collection agency. Police Officers are not Repo-persons. I had Tow Companies call wanting us to standby while they snatch a vehicle during a repossession. We do not do that. We have become what, is now created by politicians and community leaders of a policy of **"Just call the police."** If your neighbors' trash is blowing in your yard, call the police. If your neighbors' dog is barking call the police. If children are playing basketball at 2 o'clock in the afternoon and their having too much fun, call the police. If a supervisor tells the caller that this issue is not a police matter, then its "I'm taxpayer, or I know the Chief, I know the Head of the County Council, I know the County Executive." Or "Do you know who I'm." It is that I am a taxpayer that kills me. The last time I check there was no Executive Order sign by a President making police officers tax exempt. But when someone gets shot, in broad day light and the police arrive, "I don't know anything, I didn't see anything, I'm telling you anything, I'm not a snitch." But when the police must go hands on with someone, "Oh, I saw the police beating him for no reason,

Oh, I got everything on my cell phone." I have had people walk up and say to me "Oh you let them, the criminal, back on the streets." Or "Another one dies in Police custody." I had to explain that it is not police who let him back on the street,

It was either the Court Commissioner who gave him pre-trial release and or bail, or a Judge granted bail and or pre-trial release. The police have no control or say over that. There was an incident where a suspect ran over a Police Officer in a stolen vehicle. The suspect is apprehended and transported to the Department of Corrections. Several days later the suspect was found dead in his Cell. A few days after the incident this man approached me and stated, "Another one dies in Police custody huh?" I replied, what are you talking about? That guy that they found dead in his Cell, another one died in Police custody huh. Well of course I got irritated, because he was speaking on something that he had no idea what he was talking about, so I took that moment to enlighten him. I said one he did not die in POLICE custody. He died in the custody of the Department of

Corrections. His reply "Oh that's not the Police Department?" No, that is why you need to know what you are talking about before you open your mouth. So, I explained to him that the Department of Correction is not a part of the Police Department. But I got angry not by his comment, but that the only thing he could think of or say was about an arrestee was found dead. Not the fact that a police officer is dead. A police officer who was a son, a brother, a father. How hard would it have been for the car theft to just stop the vehicle a give up that way both would have been alive. Then there is that issue. The public not looking at was led up to the incident with the police officers. No one ask what led up to the incident involving the police. What cause the person to be shot by the police or chased by the police.

Let's look at the incident involving the Police Officer who shot the teenage girl who was about the stab another girl with a knife. The girl had the other girl pined up against the car about to stab her when the police officer pulled up. It was happening so fast the officer never had time to give any verbal commands. He only had time to draw and shoot. There was a man standing outside who was standing there the whole time from the point where the girl was going to stab the other to the very moment the officer fired. But then shouted you didn't have to shoot her. Well had you, MAN grabbed her went she had the knife, or stopped her when she was trying to stab the other teen there would have been no reason for the officer to shoot. But it is part of the Criminal Justice System. I am not going to deny that there are times when the police drop the ball on certain crimes and court cases. There have been officers that have not properly prepared for court, or officers that perjure themselves on the stand and lose their credibility testifying in court. There are also states attorneys that have not come prepare for trial or go for a plea then taking a court case to trial. There are 3 types of states attorney. The first are there for the title and of money or they have a political agenda. Then there is the second one who is incompetent, they are never prepared, defense attorneys quickly intimidate them. Then there is the third who are great attorneys they have their game together regarding the case and can manage themselves inside a court room. Then there are the judges. Some of them have a political agenda or political motive. Some have a personal agenda.

I knew of a judge whose daughter was on drugs and died at the age of eighteen from a drug overdose. From that day forward every drug dealer who came into that judges' court room got the maximum sentence and if they had a handgun when they were arrested, then that would be an additional 5 years added on the sentence. Then there is the judge who must, as they say, "***send a massage***" that they are hard on crime, corrupted or dirty police officers. Then it is that judge who gives the slap on the wrist of criminals who they think is a victim of society or a poor Childhood. I arrested a 19-year-old for selling marijuana inside a high school to students during school hours. At the time of his arrest, I recovered nine bags of suspected marijuana. Now when it went to court the judge gave him 18 months unsupervised probation. Now that is when they had the drug free school zone, which I do not hear anything about anymore. These drug free school zones stipulated that anyone dealing drugs could not even be in possession or sell drugs one thousand feet of any school or it was MANDITORY jail time. This gentleman was caught on school grounds selling to students and apprehended by school resource officers. The day of court he walked right out of that court room. The assistant principle and I just sat there and looked at him walk out. My favorite that left me so angry I could have spit brimstone. I had a defendant who arrested for attacking a 12-year-old girl with a Pitt Bull as the little was taking out the trash. It was at 2:30 on a Saturday afternoon. I detained him, read him his rights at which time he admitted to attacking the little girl with the dog mauling her ankle. I got him to give me a written statement of the facts. I got statements from the little girl and other witnesses to the incident. I took pictures and obtained hospital records. Then came the day of trial. The defendant shows up without an attorney me thinking it is a rap, he is going to jail. Sitting on the bench was a visiting judge from lord knows where. The guy was sitting at the defense table, myself and the state's attorney was sitting at the other table. I started reading the statement of facts, as I got down to the part where the defendant stated that he admitted what he did the judge stood up, leaned over the bench, and said to me "He told you that?" I looked at the state's attorney as she just sat there shrugging her shoulders in disbelieve. I turned back to the judge "Yes your honor." He turned to the defendant, "You told him that?" and stated, "Yes your honor." The judge dropped back in his chair and sighed then stated, "I'm sorry, I'm going to have to find you guilty." I sat there in rage. Your sorry, so had he'd quick witted enough to say, "I never said that to this officer." He would have believed him over me. Me the officer with the written confession, the victim who was still healing from the attack, my photographs and medical records means nothing, and again 18 months of unsupervised probation, no restitution for the victim's medical bills nothing. I have had judges and states attorneys throw out charges of assault or assault on police and was told "That's what you get paid for." Even a heavy weight boxer does not step into a ring to get his ass whipped. I have a saying, there is an enormous difference between stupidity and ignorance. Ignorance is when you do something or say something wrong and not know that it is wrong.

Stupidity is when you do something stupid, and you know it is stupid even before you do it. When it comes to Law. Enforcement and the Police, the public's ignorance it is what is causing the problem between Law Enforcement and the public. You must understand that in the criminal justice system there are a lot of moving parts, but if the public took the time to find out how it all works then everyone would have a better understanding on how the system works, we take time to find out how other things function in this country. You would not take your car into your primary care doctor when the check engine light comes on, no more than you would your mechanic do your taxes. Now I do specify ignorance when I am addressing this issue because they are so-called political leaders have them believe that the police and or Law Enforcement is the end all be all problem solvers of the world when we are not. When I deal with people, and they say "I want so and so locked up because......" Again, that is not how that works. An officer must do an investigation, ask some questions to determine if a crime has even occurred. To see if the matter is a criminal matter or a civil matter, and if it is a criminal matter is it something that the police can handle immediately or does the complainant has to see the assistance of a court commissioner. There are times when the victim must do a little leg work and go to the courts. Issues like second degree assaults, unauthorized use of a motor vehicle to name a few. Those are two situations where the victim must go to a court commissioner and have charges filed. But instead of saying that over the phone when they call 911 it just sends the police-send the police. Now their thinking ok's the police are on their way and when they get here, they are going to solve my problem. Then when the officer or officers arrive, they become angry when they are told they must go to the courthouse to file papers. There was also the incident that made national attention. It was a January 29th, 2021, incident when the Rochester New York Police were called to an elementary school for a distraught 9-year little girl who was subsequently pepper sprayed by police. Now why were the police called for a distraught 9-year-old? Even though it was said that the parents called the police. Now let us entertain that idea for a minute, the police on a 9-year-old girl, now I know that those parents knew for a while that they daughter had issues. Why wasn't the child referred by a primary care doctor to a mental health hospital? And if not, the school principal could have stepped in? The Guidance Counselor or the school nurse? The school could not have called someone from the crisis center to come and intervene in the child's behalf? There was no reason whatsoever that any police officer been made to handle that incident. A whole lot of people dropped the ball on that one and yes, the police take the blame. Donna Lieberman of the New York ACLU even stated, "The Rochester Police Department has no business serving as the first responder in a mental health crisis that calls for mental health expertise." Wow the one time I agree with the ACLU. Then there is the situation where they person wants to be an ass and put their once significant other out on the street. Again, the police arrive, and it is "I want them out, NOW!"

Then they again get angry when the officer tells them since they have been staying more than 30 days you must give them a 30 day notice just like an eviction, now I know this applies in Maryland I do not know if it is the same in all states. What is that problem you ask? Well let us go back before it became a problem. In what some of us call ***"Back in the day."*** I never saw the police in my neighborhood. When I saw the police, someone was either dead or going to die. In my day, the men took care of and protected the neighborhood. The women watched over the children even if the children were not even theirs. If a mother saw a neighborhood child outside past dinner time it would be, "Jimmy where's your mother?" She is still at work. "Come in here wash your hands and eat dinner, you can stay here until your mother gets home." The neighborhood watched over the elderly. If Ms. Johnson grass needed cutting the men would not wait for her to ask, they would just cut it. Yes Ms. Johnson would still try to pay but the men would not take her money but the did get some fried chicken and cornbread for their work. The neighborhood pulled together no matter what. Now this generation, this Social Media generation only thinks about themselves. When some of the commuters on a Philadelphia train sat and did nothing as a woman was being raped and the rest recorded the incident on their cellphones. But let's restrain the police. When snatch and grabs are off the hook in California but let's restrain the police. When rioters burn down stores and the police station but let's restrain the police. When a Carjacker walks up to a woman a place a gun to her 3-year-old sons head and take her phone and SUV but let's restrain the police, when Asian Americans are being assaulted in broad day light, but let's restrain the police. When a mental homeless man walks up to a nurse sitting at a bus stop and beats her to death and walks away but let's restrain the police. Its all "F" the Police until you get robbed. The social media culture. That would stop and record incidents on their phone to post it on their IG a go back and see how many likes they get but won't take that same phone and call 911 to get that person help. Then there's those who protest when the Media posts "White Police Officer shoots black man. "But again, where are these protesters when there is Black on Black crime. When Pookie kills Man-Man. Where are the protesters when a 7-year-old gets shot by a drug dealer while she's riding her Bic in her own front yard? Where are the protesters when an 8-year-old boy who's playing a video game is shot and killed in his own living room? Where are the protesters when a mother is killed by a bullet going through her living room window while she is hanging up curtains by a drug dealer who was supposed to be on home detention running through a parking lot trying to shoot a Crack Head.

Chapter Two

The Cop

Washington D.C. New York and Baltimore City and many other major cities had and currently still have what is known as ***Foot Patrols*** which was once called ***Beat Cops***. The term beat is the area and or territory that a police officer patrols at any given time. This was considered traditional policing back in the late 19th century. This is where officers are assigned certain areas of the city to walk around and project a police officer present and have a one-on-one relationship with the community. During those times. Every Beat Cop knew everyone in the Beat. The kids, the store owners, the residents the elderly. During those times, the public felt good about having the Beat Officer who they could stop and talk to on a regular basis. This encourages more interaction between the police and community members. Before the invention of police radios maps were drawn and beats were assigned to certain officers. The officer would be given a call sign and an area of responsibility. Beat officers were required to be at certain locations that were 30 to 40 minutes apart and remain at those locations for approximately 5 minutes then move on to their next location. Beat officers were commonly used in the 1800's. By 1877 Police Departments started deploying Call Boxes which were used by beat officers, officers used the call boxes to check in and or call for a Police Wagon. They were used up until the 1960's-1970 the introduction of police radios where born.

The Street Cop is now performing what is commonly known as Proactive Policing. I have been doing police work for 30 years and I have yet to find out at what point did we go from Beat Cop i.e., now call **C**ommunity **O**riented **P**olicing. To proactive policing. This practice involves having a police presence believed to deter crime. To investigate and find offences in hopes of preventing crime from happening. Some studies have shown that proactive policing has reduced crime to some degree for the short term. The other side of that coin is the effects proactive policing have on other outcomes as far as the behavior of police officers and racially biased behavior. When I first come on the police department, I was the Beat Cop. I would respond for calls for service, took the time I need to solve the problem and moved on. In my patrol capacity if I saw a traffic violation, I would affect a traffic stop. I would then find the status of the violators' drivers' record and determine whether to write a citation or let them off with a verbal or written warning. Then on or about 1996 someone decided that productivity was the only way to determine whether you are a great police officer, by the number of tickets you issued or the number of arrests you made monthly. I mean monthly, you had to be consistent with it and for whatever reason your numbers went down you were called into the Commanders Officer and explain why your numbers are down. Yes, I said it Police Officers are directed by the Command Staff to write tickets and make arrest. I am going to make this perfectly clear that police officer is not out running around just issuing tickets and making arrest because we are board. We are directed by the higher ups, and they keep track of the citation numbers and arrest numbers of each officer and each squad monthly. The same Commanders that smile in your face at community meetings. The same ones who you go to complain to about getting tickets from speed traps or arrested through crime suppression operations, are the same Commanders who behind closed-door order us to go out and give you the tickets. And it is not just one department, Departments in Maryland, Texas New York is pressuring officers to meet **Quota's** including tickets and arrest or face disciplinary action against them. What they called ***"STATS"*** are also used in officer's evaluations and promotions, or transfers to other units. The Command Staff then takes these numbers and puts them on a nice colorful spread sheet as they stand there in their community meetings a say how much they have reduced crime with arrests and officers conducting traffic enforcement.

"As you can see our District made 175 arrests in the first 6 months and issued 1423 traffic citations." An officer's numbers are low the officer is denied transfers and their scores on their evaluations are low. When you see police, officers pull up on a group of young Black men or teenagers, just do not assume that those officers are pulling up on them because their black. Best believe seven out of ten times someone in that neighborhood called. It is not like the police where driving by and said, "Hey let's go get those Black guys." Yes, again I know there are police out there that have that thought process, I have met them, and I hope to explain how and why they exist. Now back to why things are the way they are. I was working evening shift when I get a phone call from a co-worker. "Hey, the Major wants us to be by 51 Liquors and move those guys from the parking lot." I told him I am not doing it. Well, the

Major said.... Then I asked, "Did the store owner call 911 and asked us to move them?" My friend replied, No. So, like I said I am not doing it, he is the police just like I am, why didn't he pull up in his police vehicle and ask them to move? He wanted us to go down there to move some men in a parking lot who really was not doing anything but talking to their friends, the store owner did not find it a problem. Now had I went down there, got out of my police cruiser, and told them to leave, it would have taken only one to say, "I'm not going no damn were." Then what? He would be calling my bluff if I had told him I would lock him up, for nothing. Then all he would have to do is file a complaint against me and I would have been thrown under the bus because no one from the Command Staff would have come to my defense or say hey I told them to do it. There have been a lot of incidents where officers are placed in those situations by either a complainant or the department and or government. So why are there bad police officers? The Police Departments are the reason there are bad police officers. It angers me because every time a bad police officer makes the news the public looks at me as though I hired him. There has always been a problem with hiring new police officers. One of the problems was the fact that those officers where not making the standards. This started becoming a bigger and larger problem within Law Enforcement, so departments became so desperate that they started to lower the standards, so when you lower the bar in recruitment the garbage gets in. That is what has happened with agency. They have chosen quantity over quality. Departments would rather have more officers than good officers. Why because the Governors, Mayors, and County Executives who made promises to the continuance of more police on the streets.

So, to keep that promise they have made department lower the bar. I have always been the beat police officer. I know how to be a street Cop, if necessary, but I prefer to be the beat Cop. I get things done better without having to resolve a problem with arresting someone. Now there does come a time where yes, I do have to lock someone up. If I got to the domestic and someone or both parties have injuries someone must go to jail. I can defuse the situation with what they use to call verbal judo. What did I get for using the beat police way of policing? I got respect even from the drug dealers, why because I was always fair. When I arrested a drug dealer it was not because I was board and I kept digging for an hour till I found something. I got them because I would catch them slipping.

In the beginning where drug use was a reason for being denied, they let a little drug use slide. The past traffic violations, the past misdemeanor overlooked, and those people are hired. I know this. What has also made this a problem is the fact that department have hired civilians instead of police officers or retired police officers to do the background checks. Police Officer and retired Officers do detailed backgrounds, they find the garbage that try to get through. Sometimes I ask myself which is worse? The garbage that gets through or the departments that let them get through. I have known of a police officer who was laundering drug money for a drug dealer. The Federal Agents did not press charges against her because she was willing to testify against him. What I was angry about was the department not only did not fire her but when I saw her again, she was promoted to Sergeant. When I ask why she was not terminated their answer was that the Federal Officers did not prosecute. It should not have mattered she committed a complete violation of police policy as far as conduct.

Civilians just pick up the phones to contact the reference, ask a few questions and check the boxes. My background investigator went out to my old High School, talked to my old High School teachers face to face, my neighbors face to face. Because of poor background checks I have known of a Blood Gang member who almost became a police officer. I have known of a man who almost became a police officer be got arrest for kidnap-rape before he could be hired. All in the name of quantity police officers not quality. I would bet my check that even those officers who have been criminally charged of excessive force have multiple prior complaints of excessive force filed to their department. I have known of Academy Instructor who told their department that certain cadets need to be drop from the academy class, but they were told to ***"push them through."***

Within 18 months nine of those cadets were fired for their behavior or fired for criminal acts. Again, all in the name of more police on the streets, yes but at what cost? Then there are the police departments that not only hire these red headed stepchildren. But continue to keep these officers on their departments and continue cover up and overlook their complaints of excessive force.

Chapter Three
The Misuse of Police

When you're driving through that residential neighborhood and you get pulled over by the police for doing 41 in a posted 30, it is not the officer who has decided to put up the speed trap. It was the department. When you look out your window of your apartment complex and see 5 police officers detaining 4 young black men its not the police, its your neighbors. Yes, there are a few things police initiate, but not many. The many things that officers do are a result of the direction of the department the citizens or the government. When I'm on patrol I don't drive around saying to myself, "Self I have nothing better to do so let me pull this Soccer Mom over". There is a lot of incidents where to police were used for whatever reason. There has been misuse of law enforcement for decades. Let's start from the beginning.

Police misused during Civil Rights Protest of the 60's

During that time police with dogs, sticks, guns, and fire hoses. Were used against African Americans during peaceful protest nationwide by order of the state and or federal government. No police officer even if they where racist came together those moments on their own to do that to Civil Rights protestors, they were ordered. Law Enforcement was used against Martin Luther King until he was killed. Law Enforcement played a hand in the death of Malcom X. In my second book **Urban Warfare,** I tell how Law Enforcement is used to occupy urban neighborhoods. During the Clinton administration he passed a bill giving Black people more jail time for selling crack cocaine that for powder cocaine. Even though powder cocaine is more expensive. Cocaine is the base for crack. You can't have crack cocaine unless you have Cocaine. But at the time who could afford cocaine? Exactly. But I'm getting off track of my point. The Enforcement by those who are in control of Law Enforcement Officers. An officer operates by the direction of the command staff who gets their orders from above. During the direction from above, those officers during the civil rights movement had to have been given the authority to use force. They had to have been given the authority to use dogs, and water hoses. Never this some of these Law Enforcement Officers, where they are good or bad are operating on their own. Yes, some are abusing this authority but at the end of the day the order is still given, and as far as bad actors, if you go back into the Internal Affairs files of these officers you will find an incident and or complaint that should have gotten this officer fired long ago but the department skill kept them on.

Police misused against peaceful Vietnam Protestors

During the Vietnam War the American people sought to end our occupation in this police action. When the American people stood up against the action, they were met with police action. And like the civil rights era when the people stood up for a cause they were put down, all in the name of Law and Order. Yes, society needs order, that's not the issue. The issue is when those who are in charge make the command decisions on the actions to be taken against human beings. There the decisions are being made, not by the patrol officer. Even though you might not see it there are officers who refused to follow an unlawful order.

Police misused in L.A. during the Rodney King Riots

After the Rodney King trial the streets were set ablaze. Now not to come to the defense of the officers but at the time their departmental policy dictated that they were not to touch an alleged suspect unless they complied. Again, officers following policy yet getting thrown under the bus. The officers were charged and put on trial, but because of the testimony of one of the supervisors that it was department policy to use their sticks and tasers and pepper spray and not to go hands on until the suspect complied with the commands. They were found not guilty. Not because they where white, but because they were following LAPD policy. So, they walked. Now had the department had gone to the fore front and stated to the public that the officers acted strictly to policy maybe, just maybe there would have been just a protest and not a riot. But what do I know?

Police misused during the Black Lives Matter Protest

During the Black Lives Matter protest after the death of George Floyd not only police but Nation Guards where used. Now to the issue of George Floyd and I will make this clear, at no point did I condone the actions of that officer, but that was that departments police of using that technique. But that policy mandates the if an officer uses the technique, they are to check the subject every 1 minute and 30 seconds to see if the person is conscious and breathing. If the person loses consciousness at any time the officer is checked to make sure the person is still breathing. Not only did he not do that but in the video, I can see his hands in his pockets, chilling. That what enraged me about. And because he failed follow policy a man died. It was also my understanding that he had numerous prior complaints for excessive force and the department kept him on the department.

Chapter Four
The Ultimate Sacrifice

There are approximately 800,000 police officers in the United States as of to date there have been 22,000 police officers killed in the line of duty. There are those who try to rationalize the killing of officer. I've heard those who ask the question, what drives the offender to kill police? I really find it hard to believe that is a question about why killers kill. The only reason that has some bit of understanding is the fact that Law Enforcement officers are an extension of the Federal Government. And there are those who have a bone to pick with the government for some reason that they only understand. And that they know that contact with Law Enforcement the closest they are going to get to engaging the government. 800,000 is not really that many. There are, I am sure many more who applied but for whatever reason did not make it through initial processing, did not make it through the Police Academy either injury or failed to pass the exams or qualify with their service weapon or, in many cases something came up in their background check. Then there are those who do not make it through the Field Training portion. Nothing against those who failed for whatever reason they just did not make it sometimes you need ask yourself I want to be X, Y, Z, but can I? Yes, there is that textbook academy class answer to why do you want to be a police officer?

"To protect and serve." Then you are in. you have made it through the academy and now you are a police officer. You are out here fighting crime and evil. Those first five years are great. Then comes year 10 and you have gained a little weight. The back is giving your problems from years of wearing the gun belt. Let us not also forget the number of birthday parties you have missed. The number of summer barbeques. The family get together and anniversaries. And the moments you complain about the toll it is taking on your personal live you hear "This is what you signed up for." But now let us add the anti-police atmosphere. The Damn if you do, damn, if you do not attitude. Even with the advance of technology to make the job more efficient has made it harder. More officers are becoming more disillusioned by the job of police officer. And departments are struggling to retain police officers. The Monday morning quarter backs in the public and in the news media. The police department that you worked for, for so any years who you cannot understand why they are not giving you any support or the Criminal Justice System who also let you down when you watch case after case of defendant walk with probation or plea bargain. I had several cases, one I had where I charged the guy with Statutory Rape of a 14-year-old, and he was nineteen. The day of trial, 6 months later. It was me, the girl, and her parents there ready to go to trial. The defendant was brought in, in handcuffs and shackles. I ask the States Attorney if he was still in for the rape charge and he replied, "No he's currently doing 18 months for an armed Car Jacking of an 80-year-old woman." He then walks over to the defendant's attorney and their talking for about 15 minutes. He comes back and says, "You can go." I was like what do you mean we can go? He has agreed to take a plea. A plea for……??? I replied. 18 months to run concurrent to the time he is already serving. So, he is going to do 18 months total for an armed carjacking and a rape, and you are comfortable with that? I asked. He just stood there and look at me. Speaking of plea deals, another thing people do not know. When you hear some of these States Attorneys with these 90 to 95% conviction rate this number is not based solely on winning cases at trail, they, the state's attorney. Counts a plea as a win hence the high conviction rate. speaking up for all while the stress has put so much on your personal live that you are divorced or separated pending a divorce. You children are angry because you have missed most of their childhood working evenings and midnights and weekends to where they never had a normal family life. You while the media and the public are hammering you. Not having the courage to even say this officer was right or justified for their actions for fear of public outrage. Many Law Enforcement Officers face not only issues on the street, but their own issues with their personal life. Many relationships and marriages have been ruined because of it. One of the things causes stress on Officers families is tight budgets. Officers are not known to be well paid so some must cut back financially on the household budget. Which has officers working overtime assignments and Secondary Employment to make ends meet. The last department I work for I left in 1996 after being there for 7 years making $28,900.00. Then there are the times when your working holidays, Christmas, New Years, Birthday's 4th of July. There are also the issues of rotating shift work. Days, evenings, and midnights. Working during the week, the weekends. Having Court, mandatory overtime. Because of this inconsistency with the shift work puts a major strain if you have a family with children. What is Shift Stress? This is from a medical paper regarding stress.

Mental Symptoms

- **Increased Irritability and Being Moody.**

It noted especially by partners that shift workers become more irritable after working night shifts. Our survey found that relationship break up was higher in shift workers and major causes cited were irritability or being "cranky" and days of bad moods.

- **Overly Emotional.**

  "Snapping or losing it" is another symptom reported by shift workers, and this was frequently followed by tears. Trying to comfort shift workers under stress only added to the problem and then created a problem for management. How do you manage an overly emotional worker who wants left alone?

- **Too Sensitive and Defensive.**

  Night shift workers increased level of stress made them too sensitive and defensive. For example, the slightest

- criticism would be perceived as esteem bashing and led to disputes over minute details. Or as one manager put it "getting all worked up over nothing".
- **Contrary behavior.**

  Some workers were so stressed with night shift work that they became easily upset and were prone to seeing problems that were not there. When asked to do certain tasks would frequently do something different and then argue that they were right, and that management had a problem! These workers required a lot of management time in calming them down and trying to point out their contrary behavior.

- **Forgetful.**

  Forgetting to clock in or out and forgetting to do quality checks are two examples we found in our survey. Also, many small tasks that are done automatically during the day were forgotten at night and the impact of all the small tasks not done at night caused major problems.

Comments on Mental Symptoms

From the above description it shows that stressed night shift workers can almost be unmanageable. Some academics have suggested that counselling and even therapy sessions to help shift workers deal with shift stress. Considering the mental state of a stressed-out shift worker this approach would be extremely hard to implement.

Physical Symptoms

- **Fatigue/Tiredness.**
  Being worn out and tired for days after night shifts, generally accompanied by a lack of concentration and motivation, especially for any activity that requires effort or skill. But even simple daily activities can become harder.

- **Loss of Energy and Sex Drive.**
  Shift workers in our survey reported a lack of energy for doing all normal activities they used to do before working night shifts. These included activities like; gardening, home maintenance and recreational sports. Also, their sex drive dropped, but since it does for most of us as we

get older this may or may not be attributable to shift work.

- **Broken Sleep after shifts.**

  Working during the hours of midnight to five am disrupts your circadian rhythms (normal wake and sleep cycle) and this can cause you to wake during your next sleep and then want to fall asleep during the next shift. Your inbuilt circadian rhythms have been disturbed, and it can take several days for the body to readjust. Broken sleep stops the shift worker getting quality sleep which delays any recovery from shift stress.

- **Constipation.**

  Increased constipation and fluid retention was reported by night shift workers in our survey.

Other studies into shift work have reported similar findings.

- **Stomach problems.**

  An increase in stomach problems was reported by night shift workers. But some of the problems were attributed to night shift workers not eating properly. This suggests that this is one area that management of night shift workers can be improved. Insisting on adequate food for workers during night shifts. Mind you if a night shift worker has an upset stomach, they may not be keen on eating. Then of course they are being contrary!

- **Dehydration, Dry Mouths and Increases in Colds and Flu's.**

  This can cause headaches, dry skin, and nasal irritation, and make you more susceptible to any colds, coughs, sore throats, and flu that are floating around in the workplace. Our survey of night shift workers reported a greater number of sick days being taken with night shift workers suffering from colds, coughs, sore throats, and flu more than those workers who didn't work night shifts.

Other Shift Work Medical Problems

Moore-Ede and Richardson in their paper called "*Medical Implications of Shift-Work*" showed that shift stress complaints fell into three specific areas:

- **1. Sleep-Awake Disorders.**

Difficulties in falling asleep.

Difficulty staying asleep.

Chronic insomnia.

Increased use of sleeping pills. Difficulty in staying awake at work. One study reported that between one third and two thirds of shift workers report they fall asleep at least once a week on the job. And this occurs, because of the chronic circadian phase disruption, not only during the night shift but also during the day and evening shifts.

● **2. Gastrointestinal Disorders.**

General Gastric Discomfort.

Increased pectic ulcer disease, but this is only becoming significant after five years of continuous shift work. Alcohol and tobacco consumption, known as factors in pectic ulcers are also higher in shift workers.

3. Cardiovascular Disorders.

Increase in cardiovascular disease, especially acute myocardial infarction.

Comperatore and Krueger in their paper called *"Circadian rhythm desynchronosis, jet lag, shift lag, and coping strategies"* found that among night shift workers, the immunological functions of lymphocytes in peripheral blood show a circadian variation and are lowered at night.

Gastrointestinal diseases such as gastric or duodenal ulcers occur more frequently among these workers. Shift workers, in general, complain more frequently of respiratory and motor organ disorders, shortage of quality sleep, increased fatigued levels, and lapses in performance, and all this is just from shift work.

There are pressures doing this job that the public never see or ever will see. The only time a citizen may encounter a police officer is if they are a victim of a crime or a suspect in an arrest or at that moment, they might get a ticket. The only view is now what a how the media chooses to project all officers. The stress is so strong that there are officers who turn to drug, alcohol and or suicide because of the depression that this job also brings. Statistics show that more officers die by suicide than in the line of duty.

2019 Officer Deaths

Deaths by gunfire-47

Departmental Accidents-45

Medical (Heat attack) – 11

Other: Drowning- heat exhaustion-training accidents

Suicides- 228

Ninety percent-Male Officers

Ten percent- Female Officers

New York Officers-27

California-23

Texas-19

Florida-15

The data and information suggest that these suicides are stemming from PTSD (Post Traumatic Stress Disorder). Suicide is an awkward thing, and when I say that I mean for an individual to come that point in their life where they feel that there is no help whatsoever and they have totally given up. Speaking for men, we as men might have more of a tendency to go through with it because of the stigma of being weak if we admit where depressed or feeling suicidal. We are taught even as young boys "Suck it up, be a man." I too lost a friend to suicide. December 25, 1992. He walked into the woods, sat down against a tree, and shot himself in the head with a .357 magnum. We who knew him felt awful because we had no idea that he was really going through it. Every time we saw him, he had a smile and kept us laughing not knowing he was hurting inside.

Since then, I have kept an open-door policy with my co-workers and subordinates on my squad and to let them know that no matter how bad it is talk to me, they have my number to call me night or day, on duty or off. I think that when we started our career in Law Enforcement we just naturally assumed when we came out of the police academy that we were ready for anything, we were so wrong. The way you feel when you get on the accident scene and you see a dead child, and it is hitting hard because you have kids of your own. Your first departmental shooting, and you think your good several months later until you go to In-Service, and you have a flash back of your shooting during a **"Shoot-Don't Shoot"** training session sweating and shaking. I am saying this seriously and not to make fun of those who have experienced this.

If you have whether you are a police officer or not as far as feeling suicidal or believe your feel you might have PTSD and those who believe their friend or co-worker on the job might be going through something reach out do not wait and then the day comes when you come into work, and you find out that person has taken their live and you could have prevented it. You never know you just reaching out to that person could make them think twice before they take that step of suicide, or they might realize hell someone does care and then get that help the need. For those who are reading this and are going through something get the help, it is there and even if your department does not provide a depression and or suicide and mental health service fine one, most insurances will cover the visit and even refer you to a good one. I cannot say it enough. This job is a beast to do. I do and want to say thank you to all those civilians who do support what we do and understand what I and my fellow officers must do. It is sad because the public get their ideas of what police work is like from movies and television. I shake my head because they do not realize, its television. It is not real. The SWAT television shows, the NCIS shows. None of that is real. When I have people ask me, "Why couldn't the officer just shoot the gun out of his hand?" That is not how we are trained. We do not go down to the Firing Range and do trick shooting all day on targets, or why did the police shoot him twelve times? Ok do the math, on average a police officer is trained to fire three rounds then reassess. Now if you have four officers and all four have been trained the same way they are going to fire three times, and if they are good shots their going to hit him twelve times. Officers are not trained trick shooting to shoot weapons out of suspect's hands. If that officer or officers miss, then there is no telling where that bullet is going to go or who it is going to hit. So, if I try to shoot a suspect in the shoulder to get him to drop his gun and I miss that bullet could go through some one's bedroom window, a school bus anything. The public also does not understand that one or two bullets does not always stop a suspect. I had a friend of mine get into a shooting with another officer against a man who was high on PCP and was armed with a 45 Cal Pistol. They hit him several times and he told me; we could see the hits because he would step back but he would not go down. That gun fight lasted a little over 4 minutes, and the only reason it stopped is because the suspect bled out and he collapsed. There is also the mental stress a departmental shooting places on an officer. That one the call may be a verbal domestic. You, the police officer, gets there and you are trying to mediate the situation. Then at some point the husband and or boyfriend goes for a gun or a knife. No, it is on. Now you the officer must switch from mediator to police officer in a matter of seconds. You draw and you shoot. When it is all over you have tunnel vision, you smell gun powder, and your ears are ringing. Now you must snap yourself out of it to call it out on the radio "Departmental shooting, start me some units!" The woman is screaming your heart is racing and he is dead on the floor.

Police Suicide Rates in the United States

In total, thirty-nine of the 50 American states suffered at least one police officer death by suicide in 2019.

Signs of PTSD

If recognized early and treated properly, officers and their families can overcome the debilitating effects of cumulative PTSD. The key to early intervention and treatment is recognizing the signs of PTSD and seeking help sooner rather than later. Some, of the physical sign's officers should look for in themselves include:

- **Fatigue**
- **Vomiting or nausea**
- **Chest pain**
- **Twitches**
- **Thirst**
- **Insomnia or nightmares**
- **Breathing difficulty**
- **Grinding of teeth**
- **Profuse sweating**
- **Pounding heart**
- **Diarrhea or intestinal upsets**
- **Headaches**

Unfortunately, some police officers turn to drugs and or alcohol to relieve the pain and stress of doing this job. Most officers who suffer from alcohol issues do not seek help through their department for fear of losing the jobs. Drinking alcohol is common among Law Enforcement. A culture of drinking to relax, socialize or alleviate physical pain or traumatic memory. Fifteen percent of police who attempt suicide have a history of alcohol abuse. An FBI study in 2004 found four factors that led to alcoholism by Law Enforcement.

1. Unemotional reactions to daily stress of the job
2. Authoritative demands from Police Chiefs
3. Protection of Offices from criticism
4. Dangers of the job
5. The pressures of the job contribute to substance abuse, this includes.

. Marijuana

. Methamphetamine

. Alcohol

. Opioids

With the scrutiny by the public in the wake of shooting involving African Americans and negative media attention leave many goo officers feeling unappreciated. After constantly hearing criticisms from the public or see it in the media compounds the stress William Westley, a social scientist. Wrote that officers feel their relationship with the public is the most pressing problem. There is also the issue of trauma in this profession. Remember that we, first responders are coming to or engaged in situations where we see society at its worst. Officers with PTSD also suffer from depression, this sometimes comes with the constant exposure to death, the homicide, and the fatal traffic accident that might involve a child or children. Burnout, this stemming from doing this for years at a time. Going from call-to-call day after day night after night. I am

Sure, the stressors are even greater in areas and cities with high crime rates, i.e., Baltimore City, Chicago, Washington, D.C. Philadelphia, and Detroit. These areas are where officers must deal with high call volumes 8-10 sometimes 12 hours a day. The anxiety related mental health conditions, 1 in 4 officers have thoughts of suicide. Approximately 75% of marriages end in divorce, nationally 40 to 50%. There are also physical ailments that occur working in Law Enforcement having to wear the Ballistic Vest and Gun Belt. Neck, back and knee injuries. Heart disease, diabetes, high blood pressure and hypertension. The live span of an officer in this line of work is approximately 66 years old.

Other factors are the constant cortisol secretion in the limbic system of the brain which contributes to the cause of PTSD. There are additional circumstances with the constant incidents of adrenaline rushes. An officer can go to 3 to 4 calls a shift where their adrenaline levels are high like in departmental shootings, vehicle pursuits, suicides by police officer. By the time that officer's shift is over from this they are exhausted. An Officer also must deal with hyper vigilance every shift for officer safety reasons.

"This job takes a real toll. We respond to everyone else's worst-case scenarios several times a day. It has an accumulative effect on people."

-Captain Sarah Creighton San Diego Police Department-

Officers work several consecutive 10 to 12 hours. Working 12 hour working shifts can cause fatigue and reduce critical thinking skills, fatigue is responsible for numerous health problems, including anxiety and depression. Many jobs are stress full. The job of a police officer, the first responder, can mean the difference between life and death. Being a police officer can take its toll because officers are constantly facing trauma they resort to alcohol or drugs. The actions of a few have tainted the entire Law Enforcement profession. Policing now is more complex than most professions. Some of the general public feels that police officer are supposed to have their family counselor hat on when they go to a call, then 10 minutes later that officer who was the family counselor is not forced to switch hats and become that police officer draw his weapon and have to shoot that family member all within 30 minutes from an initial call for a family dispute.

"Two studies have found that at least 40% of police officer families experience domestic violence, in contrast to 10% of families in the general population," the National Center for Women & Policing says. "A third study of older and more experienced officers found a rate of 24%, indicating that domestic violence is 2-4 times more common among police families than American families in general."

The mental stress of the job, rotating shifts, poor diet, and lack of exercise are major contributing factors to health problems. One additional factor is that most officers under fifty don't get regular physicals. Many officers suffer from high blood pressure, high triglycerides, and high cholesterol. Most have no signs or symptoms, so the conditions go untreated for years, doing a lot of damage and clogging arteries.

The Oath of Office

I, Officer John Friendly, do solemnly swear or affirm that I will Support and defend the Constitution of the United States against all enemies, foreign and domestic; that I will bear true faith and allegiance to the same; that I take this obligation freely, without any mental reservation or purpose of evasion; and that I will well and faithfully discharge the duties of the office on which I am about to enter. So, help me God.

Law Enforcement Officers Bill of Rights

This bill, for now. Is designed to protect officers who have an incident in the course of their duties. Many states are not implementing polices to kill and or eliminate this Bill of Rights in order to have the ability to criminal charge officers in the event of a death resulting from an encounter with police

> Law enforcement officers, except when on duty or acting in an official capacity, have the right to engage in political activity or run for elective office.
>
> Law enforcement officers shall, if disciplinary action is expected, be notified of the investigation, the nature of the alleged violation, and be notified of the outcome of the investigation and the

recommendations made to superiors by the investigators. Questioning of a law enforcement officer should be conducted for a reasonable length of time and preferably while the officer is on duty unless exigent circumstances apply.

Questioning of the law enforcement officer should take place at the offices of those conducting the investigation or at the place where the officer reports to work unless the officer consents to another location.

Law enforcement officers will be questioned by a single investigator, and he or she shall be informed of the name, rank, and command of the officer conducting the investigation.

Law enforcement officers under investigation are entitled to have counsel or any other individual of their choice present at the interrogation.

Law enforcement officers cannot be threatened, harassed, or promised rewards to induce the answering of any question.

Law enforcement officers are entitled to a hearing, with notification in advance of the date,

to transcripts, and other relevant documents and evidence generated by the hearing and to representation by counsel or another non-attorney representative at the hearing.

Law enforcement officers shall have the opportunity to comment in writing on any adverse

materials placed in his or her personnel file.

Law enforcement officers cannot be subject to retaliation for the exercise of these or any

other rights under Federal, or State.

As of April 2015, the following U.S. states have enacted legislation to codify their own

variations of a Law Enforcement Officers' Bill of Rights:[1]

Chapter Five

Law Enforcement Crisis

There has been a mass exodus of sworn police officers leaving Law Enforcement starting between 2019 to 2020. This stemming from the Defund the police and antipolice atmosphere and the mass violent attacks on police nationwide. On top of some of the prominent politicians flaming the demoralization and villainization of police. Here are some numbers to give you an idea of the severity.

New York Police department as of 2020 lost 2600 Police Officers.

Portland Oregon as of 2020 lost 144 Police Officers.

Settle Washington as of 2020 lost 123 Police Officers.

District of Columbia Police as of 2020 lost 600 Police Officers.

Minnesota Police as of 2020 lost 583 Police Officers.

And that is just to name a few. Nationwide departments are struggling to hire new officers because of the current antipolice atmosphere. They are struggling to retain officers because officers are being demoralized by politicians and the public.

That is the oath most officers are sworn to when they become police officers. They have sworn to protect and serve the public in their jurisdiction, county, or state. They have sworn to give the ultimate sacrifice for a total stranger if necessary. This is the things people fail to realize. That 90% of Law Enforcement Officers are here for them.

Police were once considered hero's now we are depicted by the citizens, media, and politicians as Militarized Bigots. The Black police officer labeled as House Nigger or Uncle Tom who uses excessive force at the drop of a dime and violate the public's civil rights. The major portion of Law Enforcement are good officer, men and women who receive little pay and who take all the significant risk. Once were the days of praise and appreciation of Law Enforcement Officers to now being demonized or mythologized. There has been a ground swell of Anti-Police Sentiment in this nation. It has come to the point that society has now made police officers as the villain and so, it has come to the point that police officers are being used as scapegoats. In times of unrest and crisis corrupt and unscrupulous leaders and political leaders can cynically exploit the ancient and deep-rooted urge to scapegoat. To deflect and distract from their own inadequacies and evade their legitimate burden of blame and responsibility. I read an article in an online new paper that read the reasons Americans do not trust the police.

Defending immoral behavior.

1. Police do not nor have ever condoned immoral behavior. We do not want to work with bad officer because not only can it cause the death of a citizen but also cause the life of a fellow officer. People keep forgetting, its not the officer that determines what disciplinary action if any is taken regarding an officer, it is the department they work for.

. **Unequal application of the law**

2. These officers get away with murder idea. One, police officers do not get away with murder no more than civilians. When an officer gets into a shooting, that shooting is investigated in most jurisdictions as a homicide. A Grand Jury is conveyed by a panel of civilians to determine if criminal charges should be brought against the officer. Then there is the Internal Affairs Division of that officer's department. They place that officer on suspension and even if that officer is cleared criminally that still can be terminated for a departmental policy violation. So, these officers get away with murder concept does not hold water.

Complaining about how tough their job is.

3. "American's get that being a cop is difficult and dangerous job." Ok, first thing being a police officer is not difficult, it is Damn hard, and far as it being dangerous, officer is dying every month. Here is my favorite. If you are not willing to take the risk,
   do not be a police officer. Ok let us address that statement. Not willing to take the risk. Officers take the risk every day, it has nothing to do with the risk, and your
   answer is just stop being a police officer. Let us entertain this idea for a minute. If every police officer decided to quit who no longer wanted to be the police, then

who would be the police? Who would respond when you are your family member calls 911 for a Car Jacking or Home Invasion?

It is also the fact that this is a society that just does not like authority. We have people who hate having someone telling them what to do, what they can do and what they cannot hence the reason some people hate the police but that is ok to. Now what has all this caused? This I am sure some of the country and government officials have seen, a police officer slow down. What does this mean? That police officers have done slim to nothing. Columbus Ohio Police traffic stops down 80% om January 2019 there were 3,000 stops compared to five hundred for January 2021 the department blamed it on Covid, but a study found that officers are only doing what the community wants by minimizing those sorts of adversarial encounters and responding only when called. Ok the police departments and government officials want officers to be initiative-taking, but officers then must deal with the complaints from citizens.

I challenge anyone who thinks that it is easy being the police to stop what they are doing, weather its working for Google or Walmart. Quite your job and go to any police department and enlist. County Police, State Police, Sheriff Department. Your go through the Academy, you get the badge, you get the gun and you come out here and do this.

In 2013 I heard my former Chief make a speech at an academy graduation. In that speech he said that he was bumping heads with the County Executive trying to get more money in the budget to hire more officer because within the next two to three years there will be hundreds of officers within the department who will be eligible to retire and so more officers will have to be hired to absorb the future lose. Well needless to say the County Executive refuse to give any more additional funds. Then in 2018 Officers started leaving not just my department but a lot on of major departments began losing police officers. Departure of police in retirement is up by 45%, resignations by 18% in a 12-month period.

In New York 2,600 police retired in 2020, that is up from the 1,509 from last year. Demands to defund departments and with the Coronavirus taking a toll on emergency services and officers concerned about exposing their family and loved ones to the virus. Cities that had major protest and major departures of officers. Portland Police Department went from 69 to 30 for new hires. Another reason for departures is that police are asked to do too much, not only dealing with crime,

1) Mental Health
2) Addiction
3) Homeless
4) Lost dog

"We have asked too much from police, and it has caught up with us nationally."

Chief Zack of the Asheville

North Carolina Police Department

Made in the USA
Monee, IL
14 September 2026

63198306R00069